AFOOT IN HERTFORDSHIRE

AFOOT IN HERTFORDSHIRE

Compiled by

DONALD VEALL

SPURBOOKS LIMITED

Published by:
SPURBOOKS LTD
6 Parade Court
Bourne End
Buckinghamshire

At the time of publication all the walks in this book were made along paths designated as official footpaths, but it should be borne in mind that diversion orders may be made from time to time, and neither the Author nor the Publisher can accept responsibility for those who stray from the Public Rights of Way.

ISBN 0 904978 39 7

Printed by Maund & Irvine Ltd., Tring, Herts.

Contents

Introduction

Hertfordshire is an 'under-walked' county, although no part is more than forty miles from the City of London. In the remoter areas some of the paths may be over-grown or indistinct through insufficient use. Signposting is good in parts near urban areas but often inadequate in the more distant ones.

E. M. Forster in *Howard's End*, written in 1910, described Hertfordshire as 'England at its quietest with little emphasis of river and hill; it is England meditative'. The county has a wide variety of scenery; the parkland, the bottoms, downlands, gentle hill slopes, woods, canals and river valleys. There is much for the photographer; some fine spots for the painter to return to and spend a sunny day; much for the bird watcher; plenty in the right season for the blackberry picker; something for those interested in history and buildings; and more than enough pubs for the thirsty walker. The going is generally easy, although occasionally part of a walk, particularly in the green lanes covered by trees or near farms, may be muddy, and stout shoes are advisable.

The walks described in this book deliberately cover many different parts of the county. Almost half the walks start from a railway station where there is a reasonably frequent service even on Sundays and holidays.

When walking in any part of the countryside it is advisable to carry a map for the area and a compass and to know how to use them. If you don't know how, there is an excellent little book in the Spur Venture Guide series — *'Map and Compass'* — which will tell you all you need to know.

The detailed descriptions of these walks are intended to be sufficient without a compass but as a precaution compass bearings are given as confirmation.

DONALD VEALL

Location Map

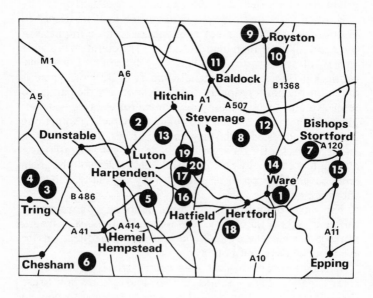

Ware

**Ware, Stanstead Abbots, Little Amwell,
Great Amwell, Ware (10 miles)**

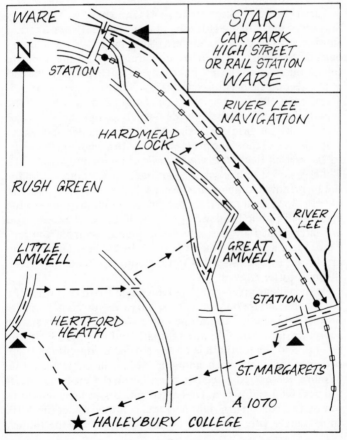

The walk can be started either from the car park in New Road (behind *The Bell* in the High Street) or from Ware Station. From the car park turn left into the High Street until you come to the bridge, where you take the towpath on the right of the River Lea Navigation.

If coming from the station, bear right past the *Station Hotel* down to the main road, cross over to the footpath opposite, which leads to the towpath, where turn right. You continue beside the Navigation (really a canal), for some two miles (E. then S.E.). Shortly after the Navigation is rejoined by the river, leave the towpath by the bridge at Stanstead Abbots.

Turn right into Station Road (A 414) and pass St. Margaret's Station. After passing Hillside Lane on the right, take a tarred entrance to a field on the left on a track going S.W. and coming out on the A 1070. Take the public footpath on the opposite side of the road on the left-hand edge of a field (W.). At the end of the second field you see the A 10 dual carriageway ahead. Turn right beside the wooden fence and down to the roundabout, go under the bridge which carries the A 10 and turn left by the bridlepath sign beside the wooden fencing.

At the top of the slope proceed (W.) with a wood on your left. In the second field *Haileybury College* comes into sight. (The College, now a public school, was once the training school for the East India Company in the early 19th century). At the end of the second field turn right behind the buildings and take the signposted public bridleway going N.W. under the trees. You are later joined by a sandy track coming in from the left. Continue ahead and, when the track forks, bear left and you arrive at a road ahead. Continue on the road (W.N.W.) through Little Amwell.

At the village green go along Downfield Road (N.) with *The Goat* public house on your left. In 300 yards you come to a gate on the right leading to an open field with a stile and a public footpath sign. You take the footpath and continue E. In the second field the footpath is on the left-hand edge. If the track becomes indistinct keep going E. until you come to a stile beside a five-barred gate. You continue on the left-hand side of the next field and over a five-barred gate beside farm buildings out on to a road. Turn right here and continue under the A 10. Immediately you come out on the other side of the tunnel, follow the public footpath sign directing you to Ware Road. You go over a stile and in another 100 yards a footpath sign directs you N.N.E. Aim for houses ahead. You pass through *Van Hage's Garden Centre* on to the Ware Road at Amwell Hill (A 1070). Turn right in this road, proceed past the *Waggon and Horses* and then turn left into Cautherly Lane leading to Great Amwell.

Great Amwell has a number of fine houses; there is also the Norman church and the romantically landscaped spring which was one of the original sources of the New River. At the end of Cautherley Lane you turn left, still on a road. Just before this road rejoins the A 1070 there is a footpath sign on the right. Take this sandy track going E.N.E. This leads to the towpath on the Lea Navigation at Hardmead Lock; here you turn left for the last mile back to Ware, going over the same route as that on which you started out.

Lilley

**Lilley, Ward's Wood, Icknield Way,
Telegraph Hill, Lilley (7½ miles)**

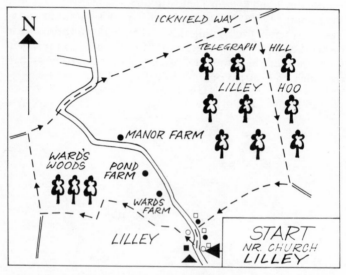

There is no official car park in the village of Lilley. You start the
walk just N. of the church and proceed along West Street past
the *Lilley Arms* on a rough road (N.N.W.), which soon
becomes a track and bends W.N.W. When the track comes to a
wood (Ward's Wood) it bends round left. Continue with the
wood on your right. After leaving the wood you are in fine open
country. In about 250 yards, when you come to a cross track,
turn right (N.). The path is very straight and pylons can be seen
ahead. After about 1,100 yards at the end of a field before
reaching the pylons you turn right into a cross track. This is the
Icknield Way. You are now going E.N.E. on the

Hertfordshire/Bedfordshire border. As you go under the pylons you come to a road. Continue ahead in the same direction (N.E.). After 500 yards when the road bends left, leave the road and continue by the track ahead (E.N.E.), still the Icknield Way.

You soon come to an avenue of trees. When the track forks, keep to the left fork. You are now climbing Telegraph Hill over chalky Downs. When you cease to climb you have an open field on your right and woods on your left. At the left hand corner of the field you leave the Icknield Way and take the bridleway on the right which skirts the edge of another wood. Care is needed at this stage as the beginning of the bridleway is not clear. The bridleway soon goes into the woods and you are now going S. The way soon emerges from the woods and goes across a field and under pylons. After some open country you have woods on both sides of you. You then come to a footpath sign to Lilley on the right. Take this footpath (W.) which soon bears S. and then W. down a hill. You can see the village of Lilley below you. You come to a lane which leads out into a road, East Street, by the Post Office. Turn left along to the road to Lilley Church.

Aldbury Common

**Tring Station, The Canal, Northchurch Common,
Aldbury Common, Monument, Tring Station (9 miles)**

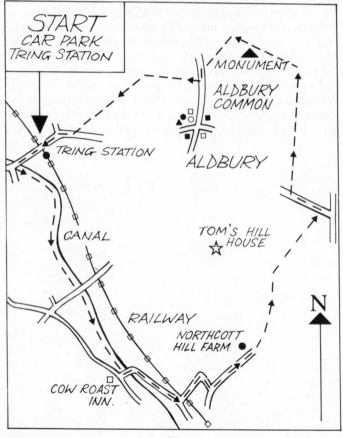

The walk starts at Tring Station where there is a car park. Turn left outside the station and after about 350 yards you come to the bridge over the canal. Take the towpath on the right and proceed S.E. with the canal on your right and woods on either side. After a mile you pass under a bridge and come to open country. About 1000 yards further on you leave the towpath at Lock No. 46 (the Cow Roast Lock) behind the *Cow Roast* public house. Turn left along the quiet road. When the road forks, keep left and follow the road over the railway. At the T junction, when you come to a high brick wall with a yellow door in front, turn right. At the next T junction turn left, where there is a *'No Thoroughfare'* sign, and proceed up the hill. At the top of the hill you come to Northchurch Common (sometimes described as Berkhamsted Common). The private road to Northcott Hill Farm leads away to the left. You take the footpath ahead under the trees (N.N.E.). When this soon comes into the open you go left on the crossing track through the woods (N.). This later comes out into the open and then eventually goes back under the trees (N.E.). There is a plethora of paths around here. Keep N.E. and you will come out on a road going W.N.W.-E.S.E. with a crossroads (B 4506) on your right.

You turn left in the road and pass a large attractive house and cottage on your right. When you reach a footpath sign you take the wide straight track (N.N.E.). You may see deer coming out of the woods and crossing the path. After about three-quarters of a mile you come to a road. Turn left and head for the Monument, a Greek Doric Column, which you see ahead. This is a memorial to the Third Duke of Bridgwater, the father of inland navigation.

Take the track to the right of the Monument with a *'No Through Way'* sign. After about 200 yards, just before you come to some cottages, turn left on to a public bridleway which starts under the trees. (The signpost is on a large tree). You proceed steeply downhill through beautiful woods (W.N.W.) until you come to a wooden gate which leads to a drive in front of an attractive house. Proceed ahead for about fifty yards to a footpath sign where you turn left and cross a field (S.). When reaching the other side, climb over a stile, turn right and in a few yards you reach the road. Turn left in the road and after about 150 yards turn right on to a public bridleway beside a modern house (first W. later S.W.). The bridleway may be heavily over-grown in the later part but finally emerges into the open where you have some fine views over the countryside. Later you see the railway ahead. After about 800 yards you come out on to a road. Continue on the road in the same direction and you will see the buildings at Tring Station a short way ahead.

Grand Union Canal At Tring

**Tring Station, Bulbourne, Startop's End, Marsworth,
Wilstone, Little Tring, Tring Station (13 miles)**

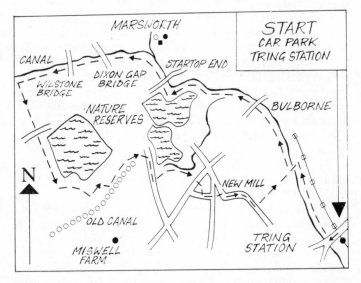

This is an exciting walk, for the most part beside the Grand
Union Canal and some of the disused sections of the original
canal. The first part of the walk has greatly benefited by British
Waterways making special efforts to maintain this part of the
canal as a show-piece, by clearing hedges and trees which
impeded access to the towpath and canal and by smartening up
the buildings.

There is a car park at Tring Station. Coming out of the car
park or station turn left and go past the *Royal Hotel*. After
about 350 yards you will come to a bridge over the Canal
(N.W.). This is a heavily wooded part in a cutting made when

17

the canal was constructed. In a little under a mile the towpath changes sides. After a further 1,200 yards you proceed under a bridge by a lock and the *Quay* public house at Bulbourne. Here the scenery changes and you see fields through the trees. You continue past the Marsworth Locks to more open country. Soon you come to the Marsworth Reservoir and the Startop's End Reservoir on your left. These are beautiful nature reserves with many wild-fowl and waterside birds and abundant marsh and water plants. It is permitted to walk round the waymarked paths if you wish.

Shortly after leaving the reservoirs you come to another lock and a bridge beside the *White Lion* public house at Marsworth. Soon the canal forks. Keep on the left towpath beside another lock and go under a bridge into flat open country. You are now walking beside the Aylesbury Arm. You pass three more locks, another bridge (Dixon's Gap Bridge), two more locks, then under Wilstone Bridge, beside a footbridge, past another lock and under a stone footbridge. The Canal is very straight here. You go under yet another stone footbridge and come to another lock where the electric cables cross the Canal. Fifteen yards short of the nearest lock gate is a public footpath on the left beside a pole. Overgrown bushes may obscure the entrance to the footpath.

You proceed on the footpath S.E. by the left-hand edge of a field and parallel with the electric cables. Keep going S.E. through four fields until you get to a road (B 489). Cross over the road continuing in the same direction as the electric cables (S.S.E.). Aim for a line of trees in the middle of a field and follow beside the line of trees on your left. After a short while you will find an entrance to the line of trees, follow the footpath under them, still S.S.E. On your left you have another Nature Reserve, the Wilstone Reservoir. At the end of the line of trees, proceed over the stiles, follow the line of trees and electric cables S. to gate opposite. Go through the gate and turn left (E.) to the left-hand edge of a field and over a stile. Turn left and keep to the edge of the field. Continue in the next field E.S.E.

A footpath sign directs you left into another field, following the left-hand edge (N.N.E.). At the next corner of the field another public footpath sign directs you round the edge of field (now E.) beside the disused part of the canal and through

18

woods (still E.). This disused canal is part of the Wendover Arm which had to be closed in 1897 because of constant leakages. The water is now moved along a piped culvert. You lose the disused canal for a while and them come to a T junction of paths beside the old canal. You proceed N.E. with the disused canal on your right and exciting views of the Wilstone Nature Reserve on your left. This path eventually comes out on to a road (B 489).

You turn right in the road, go past some houses at Little Tring and then climb a hill until you come to some white fencing on each side of the road and a footpath sign on your left. Take this path down some steps. The path follows amidst bushes. You soon come to a canal. Take the towpath with the canal on your left and proceed N.E. and then E. This canal is known as the Wendover Arm of the Grand Union Canal. After about 800 yards a small branch of the canal (strictly the Tring Feeder) runs into the main canal from the right. Take the path beside this branch (S.E.) until you arrive at a road. Turn left and cross the road and take a path through the allotments (S.E.). Turn left when you come to a road (New Road) and at the T junction cross over and take a passageway between houses. At the end of the passage turn right into Grove Road. Proceed along Grove Road past houses and then turn left along Marshcroft Lane (N.E.). After about 1,000 yards you come to the canal again. Take the towpath on your left, which is the one on which you started out. In about three quarters of a mile you come to the bridge where you must leave the towpath and take the road on the left leading to Tring Station (N.E.).

Harpenden

**Harpenden, Harpenden Common, Beesonend,
Redbournbury, Hammondsend Farm, Rothamsted
Park, Harpenden (8 miles)**

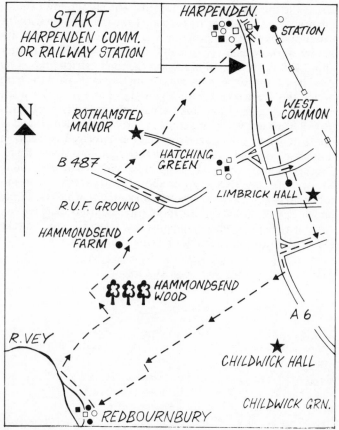

The car can be parked on Harpenden Common. If coming by train to Harpenden Central Station, at the end of Station Approach turn left into Station Street which leads down to Harpenden Common.

You proceed S. along the Common. It is not necessary to follow a defined path but keep the A 6 in sight on your right. There are some attractive houses on your right as you walk over the Common. You cross over one road and when you come to the second, having covered just over a mile since you set out, you turn left into that road, go past the road leading to the Golf Club House and then turn right across the Common by a stone pillar (S.) over the golf course. You go past a house on your left, Limbrick Hall, and cross over a road to the path opposite (S.). When you next come to a road at Bamville Wood, turn right into Cross Lane, with the Common on either side (W.S.W.). You cross the A 6, leaving Harpenden Common behind you, turn left and walk S. on the path beside the A 6 for about 250 yards until you reach Beesonend Lane on your right. Turn down here and after a short distance fork left along a lane (S.W.). You keep on this lane for about a mile and a half. You soon have open country all around you. Presently when you see a farm and houses ahead (Redbournbury) you drop downhill to the River Ver.

When you come to a ford, you take the track to the right with the River Ver on your left (N.N.W.). In about 500 yards the track forks. Take the right fork (N.E.) heading towards a wood on the horizon. The path goes round the edge of a field and eventually bends round the outside edge of the wood (Hammondsend Wood). At the end of the wood is a golf course on your right. Your way lies N.E. through Hammondsend Farm. You are now on a metalled road with a golf course on either side. Some 500 yards after the farm you come to the B 487, where you turn left and walk beside it for some 600 yards. Just after passing the Harpenden Rugby Union Football Ground there is a small lay-by on the other side of the road where a footpath sign directs you to Harpenden. You proceed through the kissing-gate and continue on the left-hand edge of a large field. After proceeding N.E. for about 700 yards you cross a driveway leading to Rothamsted Manor, a large 17th century house, now a hall of residence. You take the tree-lined road opposite (N.E.). You now keep on this all the way back to Harpenden Common, the latter part being part of Rothamsted Park.

Sarratt

**Sarratt, Church End, Sarratt Bottom, Chess Valley,
Baldwins Wood, Flaunden, Sarratt (10½ miles)**

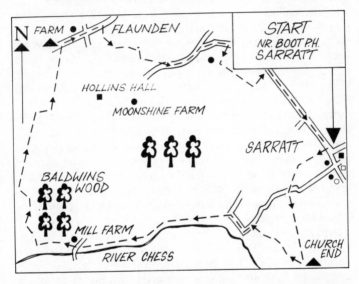

The first part of this walk is through the beautiful Chess Valley.
After rain some of the bridlepaths may be very muddy. The
route is well signposted. Sarratt is an attractive village with a
long village green between two parallel roads. There is no
official car park but parking is possible within sight of *The
Boot* public house at the N.W. end of the village. The walk
starts at a public footpath sign beside Morton's Cottage almost
opposite Red Lion Lane coming in from Common wood. You
proceed over a stile on the left-hand edge of a field (W. then
soon S.W.) and over another stile beside a gate. You
immediately take the path on the left, going off the main track,

through the woods (S.S.W.). After a few yards you fork left (S.S.E.) and soon come out to a road by Wood's Nurseries. You take the footpath opposite through private woodlands (S.W.), soon with fine views of the Chess Valley below through the trees. You proceed through two kissing-gates, on to an unmade road and then on to a made-up road (all S.). When this road soon bends left, go through the metal kissing-gate into a field with way-marked signs (S.) and soon the distinctive saddleback tower of Holy Cross Church at Church End comes into view.

The church, parts of which date from the 12th century, is well worth a visit. After leaving the churchyard you return to the field which led up to the church but follow the path N.W. on the left-hand edge of the field. You proceed over a stile by a gate and continue N.W. along a tree-lined avenue downhill with fine views of the Chess Valley before you. You continue on the right-hand edge of an open field (N.W.) and follow the footpath round the corner of the field where the path goes S.W. for just short of 100 yards. You then go over a stile on your right and continue your N.W. direction on the left-hand side of a field. You come out into a lane where you turn left and after the second sharp bend in the lane, opposite two white cottages, take the private road (W.S.W.) over which there is a right of way. You are now in the delightful Chess Valley and the River Chess soon appears on your left.

After about 600 yards when the concrete road swings to right to a farmhouse, you go over a stile and follow the footpath beside the river (W.). If the path is indistinct as the river bends away from you, aim for a small wood in the far corner of the field. You continue on the path through private woodlands and thence out into the open. If the path cannot be seen, aim for a white house amidst farm buildings (W.). The footpath comes out on to a road just short of the buildings. Continue in the same direction in the road. Just before the bridge over the Chess (it is worth lingering on the bridge to absorb the view) take the public footpath through the farm on your right (W.). Presently after going through a gate, take the bridleway going uphill on your right leading to a wood (N.). Presently the path enters the wood through an iron gate. This delightful wood, Baldwin's Wood, will be with you for the next half hour or so.

Continue uphill (N.).

At the end of the wood there is a junction of paths going N., E., S. and W. Here you turn left on the public bridleway with the wood on your left and an open field on your right and proceed W. Later you pass between two wooden posts and turn right and you will see a white house on a hill ahead. The way soon starts to descend (W.). You come to a five-barred gate with a fine view over the green valley with a road below and the village of Latimer on your left. Turn sharp right on the public bridleway and proceed N. with the woods on either side. When you come to a point where there is a crossing path and open fields on your right, turn right on the bridleway (E.). You are now out of the woods.

Soon a lane comes in from the right; continue ahead on this (E.), and pass on your right the High Top Observatory of the S.W. Herts. Astronomical Society. If you have encountered mud so far, most of the remainder of the walk should be free from it. Take the road opposite, proceeding N. for about 700 yards until you come out on to a road at Flaunden with the church on your left. There are some fine views over the gentle slopes to the S.W. Turn right in the road, go past the *Green Dragon* public house (E.N.E.). This has a garden, so on a fine day you may wish to linger a while. There are some attractive houses in this road, particularly *Oak Cottage* and *Sharlowes Farm*.

After 300 yards you go over some cross-roads and after a further 150 yards you take a public footpath on the right, and proceed along the right-hand edge of a field. You proceed into the next field by a footpath sign and go diagonally across the field (S.E.), thence between two fields, with a line of trees on your right (E.). You come out into a lane (Bragman's Lane) where you turn left. When the lane forks take the right fork and after about 200 yards take a public footpath on your right (S.S.W.). When the path ends, with a farm on your right, take the broad track on your left (way-marked on a tree) (S.E.). After about 500 yards the broad track changes direction to N.E. and comes out on to a road. You turn right in the road and in about three-quarters of a mile you are back in Sarratt at your starting point.

The Hadhams

**Little Hadham, Much Hadham, Brand's Farm, Stanton Lodge
Standon Friars, Broken Green, Wellpond Green,
Hadham Ford, Little Hadham (12 miles)**

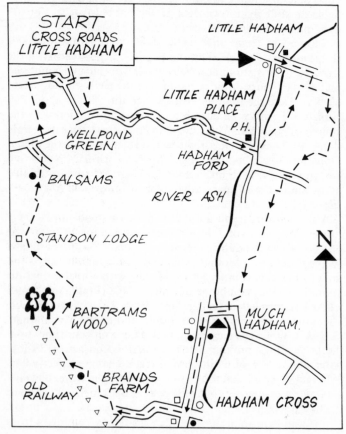

This is a very varied walk, first across open country, then through the main street of Much Hadham with its variety of attractive houses, later open country again. The walk starts at the cross-roads in Little Hadham where the A 120 meets the road from Much Hadham. Discreet parking is possible in one of the side roads.

Proceed along the A 120 (E.S.E.) for about 300 yards and take the public footpath immediately beyond the school on the right. When the hedge enclosing the school ends, turn left and proceed to a group of buildings enclosed by a hedge some 300 yards away. At the entrance to these buildings proceed some thirty yards on a sandy track and then turn right on to a path on the right-hand edge of a field (S.S.W.). Halfway along the edge of this field the right of way goes diagonally across the field to the left-hand corner. If this is ploughed up follow round the edge of the field until you reach the left-hand corner. Continue S. with a ditch on your left. After about 500 yards turn right into a tree-lined crossing track on the other side of a ditch (N.W. then S.W. and later S.).

When, in half a mile you come to a road, turn right and after a hundred yards turn left on to a public bridleway beside a thatched cottage, sign-posted to Much Hadham. Continue on this bridleway for about three quarters of a mile (S.) with fine views across the valley on your right. When you see a wood on the other side of a field, the way changes direction S.W. When you reach the other side of the field the way goes S. again beside the wood. Ignore a path going W. on your right. You eventually drop down to a road, B 1004. Turn right in this road and you soon come to cross-roads where you turn left into the main street of Much Hadam (S.). This is a street with numerous Georgian houses and 16th and 17th century cottages, architecturally very exciting and beautifully maintained.

At the south end of the main street you come to Hadham Cross where you turn right along the lane (E.). After about 700 yards, forking right just before a road bridge over the former railway is a private road (N.W.) to Brand's Farm over which there is a right of way. Here the countryside is flat but broken up by lines of trees. After about half a mile you pass the farmhouse and a small wood and continue N. by a public bridleway. You soon meet another bridleway coming in from the right. Turn left in this and proceed through a five-barred wooden gate (W.N.W.) along the right-hand edge of a field and under electric overhead wires. Remain in this field. Coming in from the left is the disused railway track. Soon your path runs beside the old railway track (N.W.). Further on the line has been ploughed over. You soon see the outline of Bartram's Wood ahead of you. At the left-hand corner of the field before Bartram's Wood turn right with a hedge and ditch on your left (E.N.E.).

At the end of the second field, still beside the hedge and ditch, you come to a wood where a public bridleway crosses. Turn left in this and proceed N.W. along right-hand edge of a field with a ditch on your right. You are going up a gentle slope. Soon you see farm buildings ahead — the first since you passed Brand's Farm. You go through the farmyard and where the road forks you take the right fork (N.E.). After three-quarters of a mile you pass some attractive houses at Balsams and come to a road where you turn left (N.W.). After 300 yards you come to a T junction where you turn right and then after 150 yards you take a public footpath sign on your left and proceed N. You pass an elegant 19th century farmhouse, bear left by the pond and continue N. until you come out into a quiet road just short of the busy A 120.

Turn right in the quiet road. After about half a mile, take the second turning on the right with a 'No Exit' sign. This is Broken Green. Just short of some farm buildings take a public footpath, amidst trees and bushes, on the right. Follow this S. until after about 400 yards you come on to a road at Wellpond Green. Keep on this road with all its bends (E. and E.S.E.) for about one and a half miles until you come to a T junction at Hadham Ford. Here you turn left and after a short distance, opposite the *Nag's Head* public house, take the footpath signposted to Little Hadham (N.E.). You cross a field uphill to a gate and stile with a wood on your right. The path curves round the edge of a field, still uphill, and when you reach the end of the field turn left and proceed N.E., heading for the church tower. Later the path goes N. and you come to a tall hedge on your left which leads to the hedge round the school where the walk started.

Walkern and Benington

Walkern, Walkern Hall, Benington, Walman's Green, Bassus Green, Walkern (7 miles)

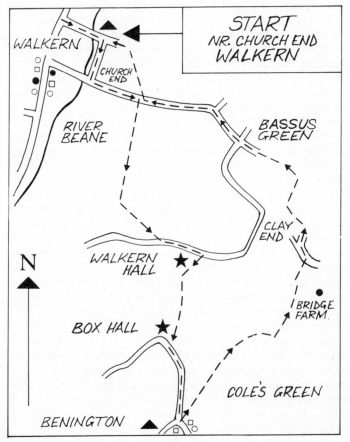

This walk covers two particularly interesting and attractive villages, Walkern and Benington. The car can be parked discreetly at Walkern in the side road leading to Church End. First you should walk down the main street of Walkern (B 1037) and see some of the interesting old buildings, particularly *Oak Beams*, *White Lion* public house and *Rooks Nest Farm*. You then proceed down the side road (E.), signposted Church End, cross over the footbridge by the ford and immediately after passing the church turn right in the road (S.) and at the T junction left up the hill. After 500 yards there is a public bridleway on the right (S.). You are at the top of the hill and have some fine views. You pass two woods (S.E.), and will soon see Walkern Hall ahead. Go through a gate and across the field S.E. towards the Hall until you reach the road where you turn left. Beside the entrance to the grounds of Walkern Hall is a five-barred gate and you go through this on to the public bridleway (S.). This path takes you all the way to the road at Benington, the latter part lined with fir trees. You turn left in the road and after about half a mile come to the village green.

This must be one of the most exciting village greens in Hertfordshire with a duck pond, possibly a tethered goat, some timber-framed well-maintained cottages and at the far end, St. Peter's Church, basically late 13th and early 14th century. After taking your fill of the village green, proceed along Duck Lane, by the pond, N.N.E. When the lane ends you soon come to a crossing public bridleway. Carry straight on down a tree-lined bridleway (N.E. and then E.). When the tree-lined way ends turn left on the right-hand edge of a field beside a hedge and ditch (N.N.E.). Later there may be a stream in the ditch. After nearly half a mile this comes out on to a sandy track, where you turn left and on reaching a road, you turn left again. About forty yards further on, you fork right on to a winding road with views of several woods on your right across fields. When you come to cross-roads at Bassus Green you continue ahead (N.W.). You are now high up and have fine views over the countryside ahead of you. When you start to drop downhill you come to a footpath on your right crossing a field almost opposite the bridleway you took on your way out. At the other side of the field you turn left down the road leading to Walkern Church and the ford.

Ashwell Station to Royston

Ashwell Station, Litlington, Royston (8 miles)

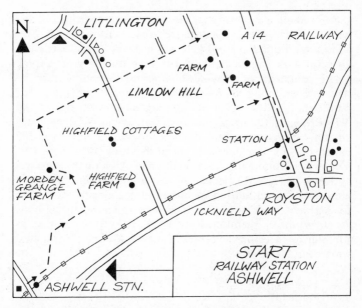

This is not a circular walk. The return journey can be made by
train in five minutes from Royston Station to Ashwell Station.
It is advisable to check times of trains before setting out. The
walk is over flat open country with occasional lines of trees
planted as windbreaks. The paths are mostly very straight and
clearly visible. Part of the walk is actually in Cambridgeshire.
Car parking space is available outside the Station.

The path duly signposted for Litlington runs beside the
railway for about 300 yards (E.N.E.). When it is no longer
possible to walk beside the railway the path changes direction

31

N.N.E. across a field. After half a mile the clear track again changes direction (E.N.E.) for a further half mile, for the most part with a wood on your left. When the wood ends you turn left on the broad track and proceed N. In another half mile you pass *Morden Grange Farm* and within a further three-quarters of a mile you come to a T junction. Turn right here on to the clear track and you will see the village of Litlington some way ahead. You now proceed E.N.E. for a mile, cross over the road at Litlington and continue on the track ahead in the same direction.

After about a mile and a quarter a road leading from a village with a church spire in the distance comes in from the left. You continue on this road still E.N.E. The track swings right and goes through a gate but you continue on the grassy track E.N.E. and in about 600 yards another road comes in from the left from the village of Bassingbourn. After about sixty yards on the road (still E.N.E.) you take a track on your right going S.E. Presently the track goes under an avenue of trees. After you have been on this straight track for about a mile, some 200 yards short of some factories ahead the track turns to the left. You proceed along this to the main road, A 14, on the outskirts of Royston (E.N.E.). Here you turn right and in half a mile come to Royston Station and take your train back one station to Ashwell Station. If you have time to spare, the famous *Royston Cave*, mentioned in Walk 10, can be visited in Melbourne Street in the centre of the town some ten minutes' walk away.

Royston

**Royston, Reed End, Reed, Barkway,
Newsells, Royston (14 miles)**

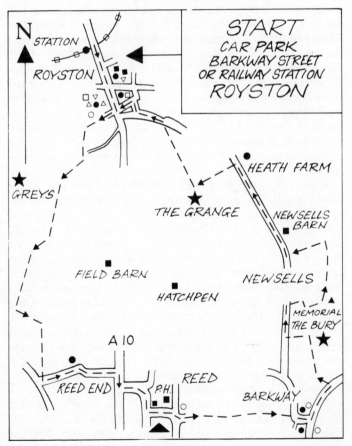

Royston is the most northerly town of Hertfordshire. It lies at the crossing of the Roman Ermine Street (going N. and S.) and the pre-Roman Icknield Way (E. and W.) both now main roads. The main feature at Royston is the Royston Cave at Melbourne Street with its ancient chalk carvings. This is open to the public on week-end afternoons from around Easter to the end of October.

There is a car park in Barkway Street behind the bus station and opposite the *Green Man* public house. If coming by train turn right out of the station into Kneesworth Street and continue S. until you come to the car park. Proceed up Sun Hill (W.N.W.). At the end where Sun Hill is joined by Stakepiece Road and Briary Lane turn left (S.S.W.) on to the track. Ignore the two paths on the opposite side of the track. Go past Heath Farm and climb uphill (S.S.W. and S.W.). There are fine views across the downs when you reach the top. When the gravel track bends right going W. carry straight on (S.) with a line of trees ahead on your right. When you come to a green triangle, bear left, first S. and then S.E. on a grass track between fields, and then E. When you come to a field, with a notice requesting that all dogs should be put on a lead, turn right on the grassy track (S.).

When you come to a road at Reed End, turn left. At the cross-roads take the left fork signposted Reed. You then come to the A 10 at Silver Ball Service Station; cross over the A 10 and turn right for a few yards, then take the road on the left signposted '*Reed*'. On the corner of the village green turn right along Church Lane and by a small building, Reed Chapel, turn left into High Street (a misleading name as it is a quiet road). Reed may once have been occupied by the Romans. It had a population of 200 at the time of the Domesday Book, not so very different from its present population. It has eight medieval earthworks. As the High Street bends left there are three public footpath signs. Two of these point to Barkway, and you take the grassy track between trees (E.). If refreshment is needed at this stage there is a public house with the unusual name of *The Cabinet* a few yards down the High Street.

Your E. direction is maintained until you come to a road at Barkway. Continue your direction E. on the road to the T junction where you turn left into Cambridge Road (B 1368) and after 500 yards, just short of a wood, take a bridleway path on your left. Keep on the outside edge of the wood and bear right when the wood ends and proceed N. parallel to the wood on your right. You come out to a small road and then turn left into another road (W.) which leads to the Barkway-Royston road. Turn right in this and continue N. until you turn right into a road signposted '*Newsells*' (E.). When you come to the War Memorial, take the road on the left and proceed N. The road continues, (but is not made up) beside a ditch and eventually you come to a T junction where you turn left (W.) to come back once again to the Barkway to Royston road. Here you turn right and proceed N.N.W. along this road for just over a mile.

When you come to a track lined with trees on your left, opposite the entrance to a farm on your right, take this track and proceed W. The track comes out into the open and then back under the trees. In about half a mile you come to a crossing path, turn right and proceed N. on this. This path comes out on to a road with houses on the southern outskirts of Royston. Continue N. along Grange Bottom and thence into Barkway Road and Barkway Street.

Baldock to Ashwell

**Baldock, Radwell, Stotfold, Caldecote,
Ashwell, Ashwell Station (12 miles)**

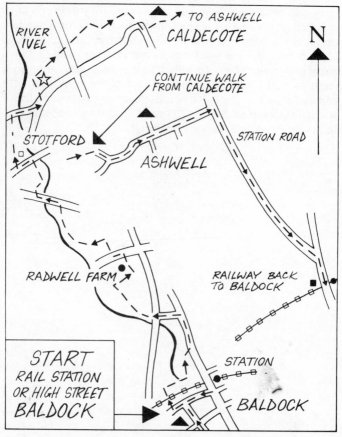

This is not a round walk. To return from Ashwell to Baldock it will be necessary to go by train, a mere seven minutes' journey on the main London-Cambridge line. The times of trains should be checked beforehand.

If coming by car, there is parking space at Baldock in the very wide High Street. Leaving the High Street go N. into Church Street, pass St. Mary's Church — a broad and roomy church worth a visit. At the end of Church Street turn left into Icknield Way. If coming from the station, you proceed down Station Approach and turn right into Icknield Way. A few yards after the junction of Church Street and Icknield Way you turn right by a public footpath sign to go under the railway. You then turn right (N.E.) on the footpath running parallel to the railway. When the path forks take the left one across the allotments on to the A 507.

Here, turn left and after about 600 yards turn into a quiet road on the left. Some 300 yards after going under the motorway (A 1) take a track to the right as the road bends left. In 600 yards just before a white gate turn right by the public footpath sign and proceed on the left-hand edge of a field (N.E.). Well before reaching the other side of the field turn left on a track running through the buildings of Radwell Bury Farm until you reach the road at Radwell. Here turn left and shortly after passing the church, turn right on to a grassy track. A worthwhile ten-minute diversion is to continue along the road until you come to a bridge. Here there is a good view where the River Ivel widens. Returning to the grassy track, proceed until you reach a field, and turn left along the left-hand edge (W.) when you will come to a tree-lined avenue. Take the footpath opposite over a small wooden bridge. Your direction is now W.N.W. and N.W. until you reach the A 507 again. Turn left, and after crossing a bridge turn right beside the River Ivel and follow the footpath over two stiles until you come out into Mill Lane at Stotfold.

Here, turn left and shortly afterwards turn right by a public footpath sign, beside a school on the left. You proceed over two stiles and come to a school playingfield where there is a sign 'No right of way across site. Please keep to the perimeter'. Obeying this request you follow right round the perimeter until you come to a footpath sign on the other side of the field. Take this path on the left-hand edge of a field (N.W.) leading into Malthouse Lane. Turn right in the road and you soon cross a bridge over the River Ivel which has superseded a ford. In 400 yards at the road junction bear left and, just short of Wrayfield House, turn left by the footpath sign. In another 100 yards or so another sign directs you right. Continue in this direction (N. E.) until you reach the A 1. The footpath may be overgrown in places but if you keep going N.E. you should not go wrong. Cross the A 1 to a five-barred gate opposite and take the footpath ahead (N.E.). Soon Caldecote Church comes into view. You are presently going to pass near this church. When you come to the end of the field, at a ditch where there are pylons, turn right and then left beside the right-hand edge of a field (E.) into the road at Caldecote. Turn right in the road and at Caldecote Manor you bear left on to an unmade-up road for half a mile (N.E.). You have fine views over open fields. Ignore a path on the right after a quarter of a mile. When you reach the end of the field turn right (S.E.) and after 150 yards turn left on a track beside a hedge on the left (N.E.).

Presently Ashwell Church comes in view. Your direction all the way to Ashwell is N.E. or E.N.E. When the clear track ends go through the hedge on the left and follow the track ahead in the same direction with Ashwell clearly in sight. At the end of the track at Ashwell a road comes in from the left. Proceed ahead to the cross-roads, turn left with the signpost '*Ashwell Station*'. Proceed along the main street of Ashwell (N.E.) — Partridge Hill, West End, High Street and Lucas Lane. This is one of the most interesting parts of the walk. Ashwell has a number of well-preserved old buildings and architecturally attractive modern houses as well as the large church dating from the 14th and 15th centuries which attracts a number of visitors especially on account of the 14th century graffiti. At the end of Lucas Lane, by the football ground, turn left into Station Road — a slightly misleading name as the station is two miles away. At the end of Station Road is a T junction and you turn right to the station some 400 yards away.

Westmill

**Westmill, "Button Snap", Aspenden,
Westmill (8½ miles)**

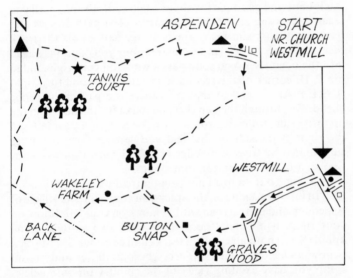

Westmill, more than once winner of the annual prize for the best kept small village in Hertfordshire, has a main street with attractive houses and cottages, including the 18th century Westmill Bury. This walk passes Charles Lamb's cottage *Button Snap* which he owned for some two and a half years.

Discreet parking is possible in the Main Street near the church. You then proceed S.W. 200 yards to the T junction, turn right and then after another 200 yards, turn left into the road signposted *Cherry Green* (S.W.). After about three-quarters of a mile just beyond an electricity sub-station you take a public footpath on your left (W.). After about 600 yards you come out on to a road having passed a triangulation pillar. Here you turn right and no doubt pause to admire *Button Snap* and fine views of the surrounding countryside. The road soon becomes a concrete bridleway (N.W.).

About half a mile after the cottage you come to a T junction where you turn left, go through Wakeley Farm and continue S.W. on a path. On reaching a wood you continue in the same direction on the right-hand edge of the wood until you come to a T junction of paths. This is the old Roman Road known as Back Lane running under trees and bushes. Turn right into Back Lane and continue for about 1,000 yards (N.W.) until you reach a crossing stream proceeding N. The path crosses and recrosses the stream many times. After half a mile the track bends away to the left under the trees but you continue ahead into the open (N.). You soon pass a wood on your right and in the R.H. corner of the second field after the wood turn right (E.S.E.). At the end of that field there is a gap in the hedge ahead. Go through the gap (E.) and make for the hedge on the opposite side, following round with the hedge on your left. On the right at the side of the field you can see farm buildings surrounded by trees and hedge. This is *Tannis Court* — your first sign of habitation for some miles.

You come out on to an unmade-up road where you turn left (E.). In just over a mile on this track you come into the village of Aspenden and on to a road with a church on your left. Soon, on your right, is a public footpath between two gardens going uphill (S.). Ignore all crossing tracks and continue S. The track is now under trees; later the trees become fewer and as you climb you have exciting views of the country on both sides.

After passing a wood on your right you run into a concrete track. Turn left (S.E.). This is the public bridleway you went over on your way out between Button Snap and Wakeley Farm. The rest of the return journey is the same route as that on which you came out but in the reverse direction, passing Button Snap, the triangulation pillar and the electricity sub-station and on into Westmill.

Great Offley

**Great Offley, Austage End, King's Walden
Leygreen, Great Offley (9 miles)**

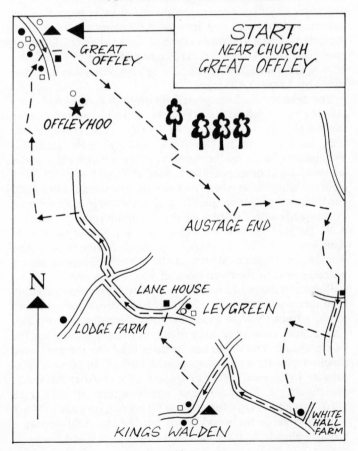

This is a walk in John Bunyan country where you will be at a height of four hundred feet or more for most of the time. Some car parking is available at Great Offley, south of the Church. The walk begins in the lane on the left of the *Red Lion* public house (E.). When the track bends away left, go straight ahead on the right-hand edge of a field (S.E.). You are in open country. Later there are woods on your left. At the end of the woods turn right (S.S.W.) across a field to a gap in the hedge, then left along the left-hand edge of a field (S.S.E.). Do not take a cart track forking left at the end of a field but carry straight on. There is a line of trees on your left as you proceed on the left-hand of the field. You are now at Austage End. Turn left in the lane and after 100 yards take a hedged public bridleway on your right (E.). After 1,000 yards turn right on a track S.S.W., later S. and then S.S.E. The end of this lane comes out at cross-roads by *Keeper's Cottage*.

You take the road signposted *Whitwell* (S.). After 400 yards take the public footpath on the right (opposite the point where the wood ends on your left). In the right-hand corner of the field turn left on to the track between fields (S.S.W.). Eventually when it reaches houses this track turns into a made-up lane which comes out into the road at Whitehall Farm. Turn right in the road and when you reach the cross-roads after 1,000 yards, take the road on the left. The next change of direction is in 400 yards where there is a public footpath right, proceeding N.W. but it is North going a little further down the road to see King's Walden Church. There is a particularly fine stained glass window by William Morris in the Church. There is also a welcome seat in the churchyard if you want a rest.

Return to the public footpath which will take you to a wood, then turn right and, after 100 yards beside the wood, you turn left on a track (N.N.W.) and pass some dilapidated barns. You then follow round the edge of the next field aiming for the house ahead. You come out on to a road. At the next road junction you turn right (signposted *Offley*). In 60 yards you turn left in the road (again signposted *Offley*). After 700 yards, shortly after a '*Road Narrows*' sign, you turn left on a track (W.). After 400 yards, turn right with a wood on your left (N.). After 300 yards the wood bends left but the right of way is straight ahead. At the right-hand edge of the wood ahead go through a gap in the hedge and when, after 100 yards, the woods bend left, carry on ahead, still N. After 200 yards you come to the right-hand corner of a wood where you can see a gate a short way ahead. Go through this gate and continue with the wood on your left for 30 yards, then bear right diagonally across the field. The path may be indistinct, so aim for the right-hand corner of the field, then go through the five-barred gate into a field beside a wood on your right. **Do not go through the five-barred gate which leads to a pond.** In 200 yards you go over a stile, turn right and you see Offley Church and the village ahead and in 300 yards you come out on to the road by the *Red Lion* public house.

Wadesmill

**Wadesmill, Rib Valley, Barwick Ford, Barwick,
Standon Green End, Wadesmill (8 miles)**

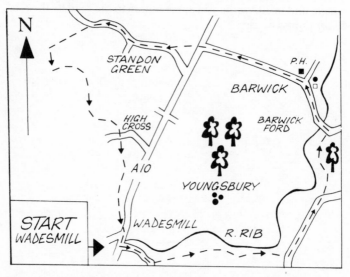

This is a walk notable for the many fine views of the
countryside. Some parking is possible at Wadesmill in one of
the side roads off the A 10. You start at the bridge on the A 10
which runs over the River Rib. Proceed along Ermine Street
(S.W.) beside the river. In a few yards fork left into Old Church
Lane. When the road bends away right take the public footpath
straight ahead (E.S.E.). Within half a mile you pass the remains
of the old parish church of Thundridge, and proceed on the
sandy track (S.E.) then cross over a concreted road and
continue E.N.E. across a field. The gentle sweep of the slopes of
the Rib Valley are away to your left. You cross over a brook

44

and turn right in a cross-track leading to houses (S.S.E.), then left when you reach the road. You ascend and now have views of the Rib Valley from above. After half a mile on the road you take a public footpath on the left signposted *Barwick Ford*. You still have exciting views of the Rib Valley below.

Presently you enter the left-hand edge of the attractive Sawtrees Wood and eventually come out at a road at Barwick Ford. You turn left in the road, cross over the river by the footbridge and continue on the road for just under half a mile until you come to a road junction at Barwick. Here you take the road that forks left, continue on this (E.) for just over a mile when you will reach the A 10. Cross over to a public footpath on the opposite side of the road. Soon you are in a road in which you turn right (E.). This is Standon Green End. When the road bends right take the public bridleway ahead signposted *Sacombe Green*. Then at the end of a small clump of trees turn left on to a track (S.). You are walking in the open country with a beautiful woodland on your left and the gentle Hertfordshire slopes on your right. After about a mile and a quarter you cross a road and take the public footpath ahead on the outside edge of a wood. Within 10 yards of the corner of a field a path hidden by bushes goes under the trees to cross a deep ditch by a footbridge. You resume your S. direction and soon see a church tower ahead (Thundridge New Church). At the end of a wood you go over a bridge on your left to a path beside allotments and out on to the A 10 at the bottom of a hill a hundred yards short of the *Feathers Inn* at Wadesmill.

Bishops Stortford

**Bishops Stortford, Stort Navigation,
Sawbridgeworth (7 miles)**

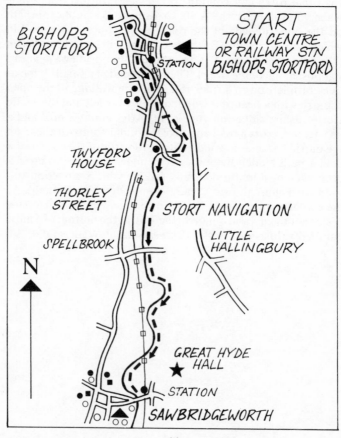

This is a walk which covers two interesting small towns, Bishops Stortford and Sawbridgeworth and goes beside the Stort Navigation. Part of the walk is strictly over the borders of Hertfordshire in Essex as most of the towpath beside the Stort Navigation is in Essex although both the towns are in Hertfordshire. This is not a circular walk — you return by taking the train one station from Sawbridgeworth to Bishops Stortford.

Worth visiting in Bishops Stortford is the Corn Exchange in the centre of the town and the nearby High Street, North Street and Water Lane. There are numerous car parks in the centre beside a park through which the River Stort runs. The towpath is best picked up beside the Register Office, a timbered building on the corner of Dane Street and The Causeway. If coming from the station, turn left into Station Road by the *Rose and Crown* public house and descend to the towpath where the road and bridge go over the river. For the rest of the walk your basic direction is S. Presently the towpath comes up to the road and you rejoin the towpath on the other side beside a filling station opposite the *Old Bull's Head* public house. Soon after passing under the railway you leave the town behind. At a lock the towpath changes sides to the left of the river. Here the river winds with woods and scrub on either side. At the second lock you cross the road and continue ahead (S.) with open fields on one side and the woods of Twyford House on the other. The general scene is placidly rural with a great variety of scenery — rushes, marsh, trees bending over the river and almost meeting those on the opposite bank, woods, scrub and open fields.

Eventually you pass a weir, go under the railway and come to the road at Sawbridgeworth. The station is a hundred yards to the left. If you wish to see the town — and you should — turn right along Station Road and then left along Forebury Crescent and on to the path beside the Church. Pevenser describes St. Mary's Church as being 'a veritable storehouse of monuments'. Beyond the church, Church Street leads to the cross-roads which are the centre of the old town. You should also walk down Knight Street and Bell Street before returning to the Station.

Wheathampstead I

**Wheathampstead, Water End, Brochet Park, Lemsford,
Cromer Hyde, Nomansland Common, Devil's Dyke,
Wheathampstead (11 miles)**

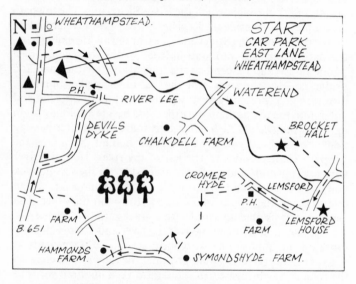

There is a public car park in East Lane behind the *Bull Inn*,
High Street. Leaving the car park turn right in East Lane which
leads to High Street. If you want to look at some of the old
buildings and the Church, turn left in the High Street, but the
walk itself starts by turning right. You go over the bridge and
soon turn left into Mount Road and go through a white gate
with a chemical works on either side. This soon becomes an
unmade public bridleway lined with trees, with the River on
your right. All the way to Water End you keep coming across
the River Lea. Continue on the bridleway until you come out

48

into the open, and at the end of the field is the Wheathampstead by-pass. You go underneath this by turning right and then left. Coming out on the other side you take the public footpath on your right up the steps, and at the top turn right and walk about a hundred yards beside the by-pass and then go over the stile on your left into a large field. The clear path lies ahead (E.) and in 1,000 yards the stile on the other side of the field is reached. Part way across the field the river appears once again on the right.

Over the stile your path continues E. You go over another stile to follow a track which comes in from the left. Soon an old house with Tudor chimneys comes into sight and you reach the road opposite this attractive house at Water End.

You turn right in the road and just before the ford over the river you take the public footpath beside the river. There is a clear path ahead. After two-thirds of a mile you go over a crossing track and up the slope opposite signposted to Lemsford. Continue ahead (E.S.E.) across a large open field to a stile just to the right of a small clump of trees. Continue over the stile E.S.E.

On the right is Brocket Park, the grounds of Brocket Hall. These were laid out by the famous 18th century gardener, Capability Brown, who also laid out Kew Gardens and the grounds at Blenheim. Two former Prime Ministers lived at Brocket Hall, Lord Melbourne and Lord Palmerston.

Continuing you direction E.S.E. you go through a swing gate, and cross a driveway to a path opposite over a stile. You are now on a fenced path with Brocket Park on your right. You soon come to a tarmac driveway where there are three signposts. You take the footpath at the right-hand edge of a field signposted *Cromer Hyde* (S.W.). If the path is indistinct, aim for the middle of the trees ahead. The River Lea then comes in sight. You go right through a kissing-gate back on to the tarmac driveway and follow the drive to the elegant Palladian bridge where you can admire the view of the lake and Brocket Hall on one side and a waterfall on the other. To continue the walk turn back a few yards from the bridge on to the tarmac drive and take the public footpath signposted to Lemsford through a kissing-gate. You follow the right-hand edge of a field (E.). At the end of the field you go over a stile and come out at the village of Lemsford by the mill. This is the scene which is said to have inspired the popular song '*Nelly Dean*' composed by J. P. Skelby in Victorian times.

In the road you turn right and after 200 yards take a public footpath on the right into a field where you aim for the far right-hand corner (W.). You go over the stile leading into the woods, and soon come into the open again. Pass in front of the imposing gates of Brocket Hall and take the path in front of a brick building beside the gates through a small wood of pine trees out into the A 6129. Turn right on the path beside the road for about 1,000 yards and immediately after the *Crooked Chimney* public house take the road on the left which goes through Cromer Hyde. After about another 1,000 yards the tarmac road ends by a collection of public bridleway and footpath signs. Take the public bridleway going S. on the right-hand of a field. Later the path goes through the right-hand edge of a wood. When you emerge from the wood after about 500 yards carry on S.W. going through a gate at the end of an avenue of trees coming in from the right. You are now on the left-hand edge of a large field; you follow this edge round with Symondshyde Farm on your left, to come into the road beside the entrance to the farm. Turn right in the road and continue in this for about three quarters of a mile. Shortly after passing a road going N., 'Tower Hill Lane', you come to a sign post indicating a public bridleway to Nomansland Common. You turn right on this public bridleway and go straight through Hammond's Farm. When you come to some dark barns bear left through a five-barred metal gate on to a track. Your general direction is N.W. The broad track ends in due course and becomes a path.

Eventually you come to a quiet road. Cross straight over and continue in the same direction (N.W.). About a mile further on you come to a five-barred gate leading on to Nomansland Common. (This was the site of the second battle of St. Albans in 1461 during the Wars of the Roses). You come out at a cross-roads. Proceed N. beside the B 651 towards Wheathampstead. You pass a delightful cricket ground on the common on your left and beside *The Wicked Lady* public house take the road forking right, Dyke Lane.

After about a mile along Dyke Lane you come on your right

to Devil's Dyke. The path runs through the thickly wooded Dyke for about 600 yards. This is probably the scene of a battle where Julius Caesar defeated the British King, Cassivellaunus, in 54 B.C. The Dyke now belongs to the National Trust. At the end of the Dyke you return to the road, continue N. cross over the A 6129 into Sheepcote Lane with the *Nelson* public house on your left. Before reaching the ford over the River Lea turn left at a public footpath sign to East Lane on to a passageway between houses (W.). Continue in the same direction across a field with allotments on your left and then on between stone posts to a hedged pathway. You can now see the distinctive steeple of Wheathampstead Church. The path leads to the left-hand edge of a recreation ground. After passing a new brick-built building the path bends right towards a lone tree and some swings. Continue on past the tree and the swings (N.W.) to the edge of the recreation ground and thence out on to a small cul-de-sac which leads into East Lane and thence into the car park.

Wheathampstead II

**Wheathampstead, Mackerye End, Gustardwood Common,
Ayot St. Lawrence, Ayot St. Peter, Wheathampstead
(12 miles)**

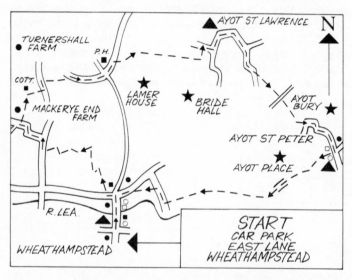

This walk has strong literary associations. Charles Lamb wrote
enthusiastically of Mackerye End Farm in '*Essays of Elia*'.
Ayot St. Lawrence is well-known as the village where George
Bernard Shaw lived for the last 44 years of his life. The public
car park is in East Lane.

  Leaving the car park turn right in East Lane and then right
again by *The Bull* into the High Street, passing the attractive
old mill beside the River Lea until you soon come to the road
junction. Here turn left on the road to Luton A 6129. After
about 100 yards turn right into Rose Lane. When the lane ends,

after about half a mile, you take the bridleway ahead (N.N.E.). After a further half mile, where there is a collection of public footpath signs, turn sharply left on the clear path ahead (W.). Eventually you drop downhill to a quiet road at Marshall's Heath.

Turn right in the road and then left along the road signposted '*Mackerye End*'. Just before you reach a road junction on the left there is a public footpath sign on the right. Before proceeding on the footpath make a short detour for a few yards down the road on the left to admire the 17th century house, *Mackerye End*, with its Dutch gables and elaborate chimney stacks. You return to the footpath which goes behind Mackerye End Farm. When you come to a gap in the hedge on your left, opposite '*Holly Bush Cottage*', you turn on to the road and continue your forward direction a few yards where you will see a public footpath sign. The footpath here is between trees and bushes (N.E. and E.N.E.). After about 500 yards you come out into a quiet road where you turn left for 300 yards. Then turn right on to a footpath (E.) which leads out to the road at Blackmore End. You turn right in the road and soon come to Gustardwood Common.

Continue N.E. over the cross-roads and take a public footpath on the right opposite the *Cross Keys* public house. You proceed on this footpath over four fields, the latter two with a wood on your right (general direction N.E. and E.). At the end of the fourth field you turn right over a double stile and then after about thirty yards over another stile ahead. You go through two more fields and at the left-hand edge of the second field take the stile on your left going into a wood where there is a public footpath sign. The path through the wood brings you out into the road where you turn right for Shaw's Corner.

Here at Ayot St. Lawrence you turn left in the road, go past the ruins of the old church, the Old Rectory, some Tudor cottages, the Post Office and Brocket Arms. At the next road junction take the road signposted to Wheathampstead. After passing *Forge Cottage* take a public bridleway on the left. You now cross three fields (S.E.) in open country. You cross over a road and continue on the clear path ahead (S.E.) and through another three fields until you come out in the road by a house. Turn left in the road. In about half a mile, just short of Ayot St.

Peter Church with its ornately designed clockface, take a public bridleway on your right, through the woods. Soon when the path forks, take the right one on the edge of the woods (W.S.W.). This path comes out on to a broad sandy track, a disused railway. You keep on this delightful track for about two and a half miles until you come to the newly constructed Wheathampstead by-pass. Here the track ends for the time being. Turn right and walk for about 400 yards beside the by-pass until you come to a road coming in from Codicote. Cross over the by-pass and pick up the disused railway track again. Continue to the end where you meet the by-pass again. Here turn left and at the roundabout turn left into the High Street. Then you soon come to East Street and the car park.

Bayford

**Bayford, Blackfan Wood, Tylers Causeway,
Little Berkhamsted, Bayford (9½ miles)**

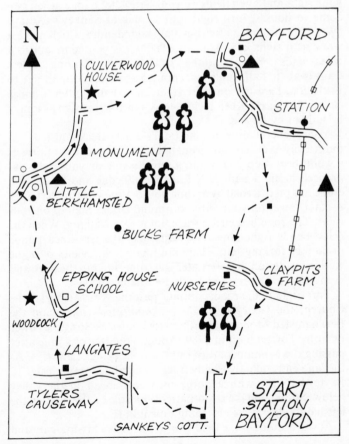

The walk starts at Bayford Station. Parking is possible near the station. You turn right into the road from the station and go W. for 400 yards where you take a public bridleway on your left through the woods (S.). After half a mile, when you come to an open part just before a cottage, take the grass track forking right.

In another half mile you will reach a road almost opposite Kingfisher Nurseries. Turn left in the road and after 600 yards, opposite Claypitts Farm, turn right along a tree-lined unmade-up road (S.W.). Here the going is good. You have a wood on your right and open fields on your left. After a mile, when you come to houses, turn right into a track at Sankey's Cottage (W.). This has bush after bush of rhododendra which make a wonderful sight in season. In 1,000 yards you come out to a cross-roads. You continue straight ahead along Tylers Causeway. In half a mile you come to a public footpath sign to Little Berkhamsted on your right immediately after a house called 'Langates'. Keep a close look-out for this sign as it may be hidden by bushes.

Your general direction as far as Little Berkhamsted, 1¼ miles away, is N. You go through three fields and in the third, as a wood begins on your right, go over a stile on your right and proceed along a path N.N.E. between hedge and fence. You come out on to a road by a white house. Here you turn left, pass a water tower on your left and Epping House School on your right. The road becomes a track but is easy walking. When the track bends right after 500 yards take the tree-lined public bridleway forking left. There are fine varying views over the wooded valley on the left. Later you come out into the open and eventually to the road at Little Berkhamsted.

Turn right in the road, continue past the War Memorial, the Church, the Georgian *Little Berkhampsted House* and the Berkhamsted Monument (otherwise known as Stratton Tower or Folly Tower) built in 1789. About a quarter of a mile after passing the Monument turn right into Stockings Lane (E.). As the lane ends take the sandy track by a public footpath sign to Bayford (N.E.) with a gorgeous wood ahead in the valley below. Soon you take a footpath over a stile on the right on the left-hand edge of a field going downhill (E.).

At the bottom of the field you go through a kissing-gate and over a stile and along the right-hand edge of a field beside woods. You then turn right into the woods to go over a footbridge. Continue in the same direction over a crossing track and up a steep slope and thence out of the woods. Here you turn right, go across a big field to a line of trees opposite (E.). At the other side of the field turn right (S.S.E.). Follow the edge of the field round, then over a stile and turn right. (You can now see Bayford Church). Turn left across the field (E.) and out into the road where you turn right, pass the church, and just before the *Bakers Arms* public house you turn left into the road signposted *Brickendon* and in half a mile you are at Bayford Station.

Ayot St. Lawrence I

**Ayot St. Lawrence, Kimpton, The Hoo,
Kimpton Mill, Codicote Bottom, Codicote,
Pulmore Water, Ayot St. Lawrence (12 miles)**

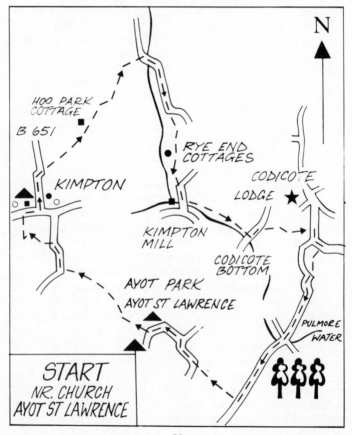

Parking is usually possible in the village of Ayot St. Lawrence.

You take a public footpath signposted to Kimpton at the corner of the road just S.W. of the remains of the old church. You go through a wooden kissing-gate on to a path going N.W. across a field. Ahead you see the new church built in 1778–79 to replace the old one. The present church has an imposing Grecian front, from which you may expect to find a large interior, so the small church inside comes as an anti-climax.

The walk continues through the gate at the end of the field with the wood on your left. **Do not take the path on the other side of the barbed wire fence.** Pass a gate leading into the wood near a water tower — **ignore this.** In the left-hand corner of the field you go through a five-barred wooden gate and follow the path ahead through a beautiful wood (N.W.). Soon you traverse a stile where the path becomes open with a wood on either side mainly of fir trees. You eventually proceed up a slope to a stile and come out into the open fields which provide an exciting contrast to the woods. The path continues straight ahead (N.W.). If the path is indistinct aim for a line of trees ahead. Eventually you will see the spire of Kimpton Church ahead (N.). The path gradually becomes a track and comes out into a quiet road.

Here you turn right. After 200 yards you come to a public footpath sign to Kimpton. Take this path, which winds very much but always keeps to the edge of the field. You eventually come to a stile on your right which leads into a recreation ground. You proceed on the left-hand edge of the recreation ground with Kimpton Church ahead (N.) into a road at Kimpton. You turn right in the road, pass an attractive house '*The Old White House*' and the *White Horse* public house on your left. You turn left on to the B 651 (signposted Whitwell and Hitchin). The pavement soon becomes a footpath going through the churchyard. You continue N. on the road and once out of the village you come, on your right, to a public footpath sign to Hoo Farm and Whitwell. You go through a five-barred white gate on a made-up private road with open fields on either side. After about three-quarters of a mile you come to Hoo Park Cottage on your left and an avenue of tall trees. After passing through another white gate, the road forks and you take the left fork with parkland on either side. This used to be part of the grounds of a country house known as *The Hoo* which was demolished in 1958. The grounds were said to have been laid out by the famous 18th century gardener Capability Brown. You come out at a road — Codicote to Whitwell.

Here you turn right. After about three-quarters of a mile you pass an entrance to *The Hoo*, go over a bridge and come to a public bridleway sign on the right. Proceed along this bridlepath (S.) and the River Mimram soon comes in from your right. At *Rye-End Cottages* you take the left fork with a wood on your right and open fields on your left. After about three-quarters of a mile this joins a road coming in from the left. Continue ahead (S.) with watercress-beds on your right. About 50 yards short of Kimpton Mill on the Kimpton-Welwyn road there is a bridleway on the left going through the woods. After three-quarters of a mile on this bridleway you arrive at Codicote Bottom.

Here you turn left in the road up the hill and after sixty yards you find on the right a public footpath sign to Codicote. You climb up the path and after about 400 yards emerge into the open. You contnue E., ignoring two tempting paths on your right, and continue to a smaller path going up a steep slope between two trees. At the top of the hill you come to a stile and out into the open. Follow the path E. between wire fencing to houses ahead. You soon pass houses on your left and go through a five-barred gate. With a school on your left you continue on a hard path between close-boarded fencing and out into a road, where you turn right and shortly afterwards take the left fork along Cowards Lane. In about fifty yards take a public footpath on your right and after going along a small road with houses on either side proceed over a stile into a field and aim for the far left-hand corner. Go over a stile and then forty yards ahead over another stile, taking the footpath (S.) straight ahead over a field to a road where overhead wires can be seen. Turn left in the road. You are now quite high up, surrounded by fields, with no sign of habitation.

After about 1,000 yards (S.S.W.) you come to a place where the River Mimram runs under the road at Pulmore Water, and a cross-roads. Continue ahead for about a further 1,000 yards and, after passing some woods on your left, you will come to public bridleway signs on both sides of the road. Take the

bridleway on the right signposted Ayot St. Lawrence (N.W.).
You go across three open fields and come out into a road where
you continue in the same direction into Ayot St. Lawrence and
soon find yourself at the *Brocket Arms*.

Ayot St. Lawrence II

**Ayot St. Lawrence, Ayot St. Peter,
Hunter's Bridge, Shaw's Corner,
Ayot St. Lawrence (6½ miles)**

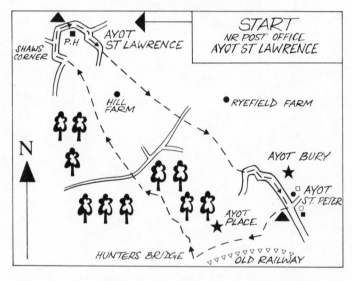

This is a short walk best undertaken in the morning when
parking is usually available in the road by the Post Office and
Brocket Arms, Ayot St. Lawrence. The first part of the walk is
the same as that described in the latter part of Walk 17 from the
point where you arrive at Ayot St. Lawrence. When you arrive
on the broad sandy track which is the disused railway, you
continue on that track for about 1,000 yards (W. and S.W.)
until you come to a bridge, Hunter's Bridge, with railings on the
right-hand side. Below the bridge you will see a path going N.
Make your way down to this. The path continues on the left-

62

hand edge of a field and then through woods for a short while and out on to the right-hand edge of a field with woods on your right (N.W.). Eventually you go through a gate and the path continues between wire fencing until you come to a road. You cross the road and take the public bridleway opposite, signposted Ayot St. Lawrence, on the left-hand edge of a wood. When the bridleway comes out of the wood it continues N. on the right-hand edge of another wood and again out into the open. Finally the bridleway comes out on to a road where you continue N. past Shaw's Corner into the village of Ayot St. Lawrence.